THE USE AND ABUSE OF TITLES IN THE CHURCH

I0121982

Daniel SHU, Eric Tangumonkem,
Emmanuel O.Nuesiri, Patrick Tamukong,
Martin Tem, Julius Ngwendson,
Hermann P.P. Donfouet

ISBN 10:0991622561
ISBN 13: 978-0-9916-225-6-6

Library of Congress Catalog Card Number: 2014934214

DEDICATION

We dedicate this book to The Most High God (El-Elyon), creator and sustainer, supreme watcher, redeemer and judge, to whom we bow in worship!

TABLE OF CONTENTS

Acknowledgement

This book was inspired by the writing of Brother Martin Tem in the yahoo groups pages of the friends of Full Gospel Mission (FGM) Cameroon *<fullgospelfriends@yahoogroups.com>*, friends of The Apostolic Church Cameroon (TACC) *<tacc-friends@yahoogroups.com>*, and friends of the Deeper Christian Life Ministry Cameroon (DCLM-CM) *<deepers@yahoogroups.com>*. More specifically his passionate writing on the multiplicity and maniacal craze for titles among ministers of the gospel, both young and old, in Cameroon. The issue resonated deeply with the many members of the online discussion forums, and eventually led to this publication that attempts to capture our convictions. It's our pleasure to share these convictions with a much broader audience in Cameroon, the African continent, and the world at large.

A word of thanks to Julius Ngwendson, a contributor to this volume, for expertly moderating the online discussions, for calling for a book on this topic, and for bringing together this group of authors. Thank you

Daniel Shu for accepting the invitation to contribute to this work, and for your wise counsel all through the preparation of the manuscript. A very big thank you to Patrick Tamukong, Eric Tangumonkem, and Hermann Donfouet for staying the course for almost 3-years from when they submitted the first draft of their Chapters to this published version. Martin Tem, it was your passionate articulation of this worrisome development that inspired this work, thank you for boldly speaking out about this, more grace to your ministry.

We would like to thank all who contributed in preparation of this manuscript, in discussions, in reviewing, and in editing this work, namely Jennifer Wong, Norman Hubbard, Mac Burberry, and Bryan Zarpentine. We are grateful to Eric Tangumonkem who in addition to contributing to this volume, oversaw the publication process. We will not leave out our wives, who encouraged us and stood by us all the way. It is our hope that our children will grow up to read this and imbibe its valuable lessons as they too walk humbly before the Almighty God.

To the reader, we do not pretend to have said all there is to say about the use and sometimes abuse of titles in Christendom. Our experience is limited primarily to what we have observed in a few African countries, and to a lesser extent our observations in the United Kingdom and the United States of America. It is our hope nevertheless that our observations and convictions will be helpful to Christians everywhere who seek to also walk humbly before the Almighty God. We believe that "God opposes the proud but shows favor to the humble." (1 Peter 5:5 NIV)

Where this work offends, please forgive us; where it is a blessing, praise God.

Emmanuel O. Nuesiri
Urbana-Champaign, Illinois, USA
12 November, 2015

CHAPTER 1

TITLES IN CHRISTENDOM

My name is Daniel Shu, I am a medical doctor and served as the Francophone African Director of Haggai Institute for 12 years, from 2002 to 2014. One of my responsibilities was to select quality leaders and recommend them for international training in the USA and Asia.

Daniel Shu

More than once I mistakenly recommended people I met at conferences who had falsely introduced themselves to me as doctors. Counting on their Christian integrity, I took them for either medical doctors or PhD holders. In the first case, the brother was a university dropout, and in another case he had not even stepped into a university classroom. My mistake was a blessing to them because they were invited for the training. It turned out to be good for them; however, genuinely speaking, as Christians, is it not a lie to carry a title you don't deserve and didn't earn?

Titles obviously open doors! When I started writing several years back, I thought it was humility not to mention in my books that I was a medical doctor. However, an elderly brother advised me not to shy away from that because readers would take my writing more seriously once they realized I was an intellectual. I believe that his advice has paid off. I have a more attentive audience, not only because of the quality of my writing, but also because my audience knows I am an M.D. In Africa for sure, and probably on other continents, the average person holds professional titles in high regard. Unscrupulous people have attempted to take advantage of this, even in the Christian milieu, by abusing titles. Is it not obvious that the worth of a person does not consist in his title but in his tenure, not in his pompous presentation but in his product, not in his label but in his accomplishment? The proof of authentic leadership is character, commitment, competence, and content. The greatest leader of all time, the Lord Jesus, said, *'you will know them by their fruits'* and not by their titles.

Professor Zachariah Tannee Formum, of blessed memory, one of the greatest African apostles of our days, was simply called 'Brother Zack.' Some contemporary mega-church and anointed ministers like David Yonggi Cho, with the largest church in the world, Rick Warren, who is world-renowned for his church and best-seller, *The Purpose-Driven Life,* and John Maxwell, with an internationally influential leadership ministry, to mention a few, do not bother about titles. John Wesley, the pioneer of the Methodist church, Charles Spurgeon, who shook Britain and the world in his time, John Calvin, the great theologian, Martin Luther, the German reformer, and Watchman Nee, one of the greatest name in Chinese church growth, did not carry lofty titles before their names. They deserved such but understood that a man's worth before God is not in labels but in his Christ-likeness, single-heartedness, and eternal impact. Today, in running after vain titles, are we becoming more spiritual or more carnal? It isn't titles that honor men—performance does. Someone once said, "Titles are granted or inherited, nobility isn't." Let us strive towards that which matters most.

WHERE HAVE WE GONE WRONG?

Several years back in our Radiology department in France, the medical doctors in specialization took it upon themselves to identify the lecturer with the most titles attached to his name and compare it with his or her performance. They found out that the concerned was the most unpopular and incompetent lecturer. He thought he would compensate for his weaknesses with titles, but unfortunately it became a real mockery in the department. Why do people run after or hide behind titles? Below are some acceptable and unacceptable reasons.

Titles open doors

I learned from my missionary pastor to use my title of 'Doctor' to prevent police molestations on the road. Each time he was stopped by the police, he would introduce himself as 'Pastor ...' and would start evangelizing them and giving them tracts. They would be completely disarmed from seeking for a bribe. In a contrary manner, a brother who was an ordained bishop without a church or a following confided in me that he went in for the title in order to have access to places he would not have without it.

Titles serve as identity

There is a normal societal convention for persons of specific categories to be known in their portfolios. Hence, medical doctors and PhD holders attach the prefix Dr. to their names, presidents of nations and ministers of the government are known as 'His/Her Excellences,' and parliamentarians and senators are known as 'honorable.' In the Christian circles, the Bible uses words like 'servant of God,' 'man of God,' 'elders' or 'bishops,' and 'deacons' to mention a few. The titles Reverend, Arch-bishop, Cardinal, Pope, Doctor of the word, Most Holy father, His lordship, etc. are man-made or biblically reserved for God. Many take pleasure in affixing the titles pastor, evangelist, prophet, apostle, or doctor of the word to their names in order to indicate their area of calling. It must be emphasized that the Bible never meant these ministerial functions to serve as titles; instead, they are meant to indicate the specific areas of individual callings. However, societal deformation has disorientated many to pleasurably use such titles for personal benefits. Charles Dickens once said, "There are some promotions in life, which, independent of the more substantial rewards they offer, acquire peculiar value and dignity from the coats and waistcoats connected with them. A field-marshal has his uniform; a bishop his silk apron; a counselor his silk gown; a beadle his cocked hat. Strip the bishop of his apron, or the beadle of his hat and lace; what are they? Men. Mere men. Dignity, and even holiness too, sometimes, are more questions of coat and waistcoat than some people imagine."

Titles often hide incompetence

Today in several African countries, charlatans title themselves 'doctors,' and some even go as far as calling themselves professors. Servants of God give themselves lofty titles, including the right reverend, the patriarch, general of God, and many more, as the list goes on. Those that do so forget that genuine respect does not come from our accolades but from who we are. People do not care about who you are until they know how much you care. Titles can blindfold in the short term, but your true worth is revealed in the long run.

Titles expose a megalomania complex

Titles help to draw attention that results in prestige and self-aggrandizement. Many of the people I have seen that care so much about titles and run for them are proud and conceited. The Bible adjures in Proverbs 16:18 that "pride goes before destruction, and a haughty spirit before a fall."

Titles often portray lack of integrity

Unmerited titles are a lie that one carries around before his name. Non-believers may play around with deceit, but how can an authentic Christian pretend to be what he or she is not? I know many Christian leaders who have bought honorary Doctorates; others have claimed titles with no ministerial evidence. Others attach 'Dr.' to their names with the pretense that they are doctors of the Word of God. Where have we kept our consciences?

Titles may portray a character flaw

I served some time ago in a ministry with someone who accumulated as many titles as he could. He was Reverend, Pastor, Bishop, and Apostle. Unfortunately, I observed his ministry for several years. While the churches of his peers grew in the thousands and franchised, his struggling assembly relocated several times for lack of identity. People left the church for greener pastures, it finally shrunk into an irreversible paralysis, and the man himself hit a stroke. Character speaks gently and longer, whereas titles speak loudly but are short-lived if untrue. Do your titles match your reputation and character? If you have no answer now, do not bother; time will tell.

When we use carnal methods like titles to open doors and receive honors and recognition, we should also understand that there is no spiritual profit. Deep calls for deep; spirituality calls for spirituality. Both God and Satan respect anointing and not titles. That is why some so-called ministers have to go to under hidden heathens to get power that would confirm their titles.

ARE TITLES USELESS?

If titles were useless, then they would not even exist. Everything that exists has an importance in the proper context. In conventional circles, titles are important for the political, economic, educational, and cultural leadership spheres. There are many settings where professional credentials give assurance to society that a leader has been properly trained and can be trusted in his field. However, as Christians, we should avoid an arrogant spirit and remain humble even in situations where we feel our titles are not being properly recognized. I heard once that a young man who had just earned his doctorate degree was addressed by a friend simply as Mister and almost caused a disruption at the degree award ceremony. He felt that he rightly deserved the title and wanted to be honored as such.

In the Bible, Jesus, the Lord of the Church, has several titles: Lord of Lords, King of Kings, Savior, The Bright and Morning Star, The Everlasting Father, the Prince of Peace, The Lion of Judah, the Lily of the valley, etc. I bet you He deserves all of them and much more. However, you would realize that he never gave himself any of the titles, nor sought after them. He is God, and even if he did seek the titles, there would absolutely be no fault in that. All the titles are given by God, the Father to our Lord and Master, who left His throne in heaven, humbled himself and for 33 years took the form of his creation – man. He neither lorded it over his creation nor made specific demands to live as a man. He humbled himself to accept the worst death in humanity: death on the cross.

The Bible then admonishes, "Therefore God also has highly exalted Him and given Him the name which is above every name, that at the name of Jesus every knee should bow, of those in heaven, and of those on earth, and of those under the earth, and that every tongue should confess that Jesus Christ is Lord, to the glory of God the Father" (Philippians 2:9-11 NKJV). Jesus' humility was the path to exaltation; we should learn from him.

Christ, the founder of the Christian faith, underscores in the Bible that ministers of the gospel are not supposed to be identified by titles but by their fruit, as it says in Matthew 7:16 and 20, "You will know them by their fruits ... Therefore by their fruits you will know them," as well as in John 15:16, "You did not choose Me, but I chose you and appointed you that you should go and bear fruit, and that your fruit should remain, that whatever you ask the Father in My name He may give you." Jesus never gave his disciples or followers titles per se. Mark says that Jesus called the 12 to become apostles (Mark 3:13-15); however, this indicated their ministerial functions not positional titles. Jesus called his disciples "friends," again not as a title but a relational appellation. In fact, Jesus warned his followers not to be like the Pharisees in seeking after titles:

> *But they do all their deeds to be noticed by men;*
> *for they broaden their phylacteries and lengthen*
> *the tassels of their garments. They love the place*
> *of honor at banquets and the chief seats in the*

synagogues, and respectful greetings in the market places, and being called Rabbi by men. But do not be called Rabbi; for One is your Teacher, and you are all brothers. Do not call anyone on earth your father; for One is your Father, He who is in heaven. Do not be called leaders; for One is your Leader, that is, Christ. (Matthew 23:5-10, NASB)

Jesus, our Savior, was not interested in titles, and he warned his disciples not to seek them. He was more concerned that they bear testimony of their relationship with him.

BE GENUINE

Let your titles be genuine and not false; let them be hard earned from toil and sweat. Let your titles match your performance and character. Non-believers may be false and go unnoticed, but God's servants cannot. Even when society stoops before you and the pomp and pageantry of undeserved accolades surrounds you, our Holy Father looks from above with a grim gaze and demands, "would my servant use the false to fight the good fight? Can he/she use falsehood to please a Holy God of integrity? Has he/she forgotten that my requirements are 'You shall be holy, for I the LORD your God am holy?'" (Leviticus 19:2, 11:44; 1 Peter

10

1:16). Instead of allowing the world to influence us with what is false, undeserving, and untrue, let us, by our integrity, simplicity, and holiness, influence our world by our fruits and products.

CHAPTER 2

HISTORY OF USE OF TITLES IN THE CHURCH

C hristianity has been permeated with numerous titles such as elder, bishop, cardinal, pope, pastor, arch bishop, shepherd, evangelist, prophet, your eminence, superintendent, overseer, supreme pontiff, father, his holiness, successor of Peter, bishop of Rome, and of course the Vicar of Christ. Although the list is almost

Eric Tangumonkem

endless, the most significant divide is that of clergy and laity. How the church got to this point of two classes of Christians is an important question that needs to be understood and addressed. The general understanding is that there are two classes of people in Christendom with two distinct functions: "the Clergy," whom all these titles apply to, and "the Laity," whose members are expected to address the clergy using these titles.

Before the establishment of the modern day church, people worshipped God and offered sacrifices to Him even though they had no special titles. Abraham, Isaac, and Jacob each built altars and offered sacrifices to worship God. These men did not bear any special title, yet they were able to offer sacrifices to God without any restriction. According to most scholars, the early church in Jerusalem was organized in the same way as the synagogue, which had a council of elders that was in charge of it.

This chapter will look at how titles in the Church have evolved from functional to positional; that is, from an emphasis on stewardship and servant hood for the benefit of God's people to that of power, wealth, control and influence for the benefit of the minister. When the Old Testament speaks of prophets, judges and kings, and the New Testament speak of apostles, elders and bishop, the emphasis is on the quality of servant leadership they should exhibit in their ministry to God's people, not on the self-promoting, arrogant pride some attach to these functions in many Churches today.

TITLES IN THE OLD TESTAMENT

Before the fall of man in the Garden of Eden, Adam, the first man, had a fellowship with God. He had no special title and there was no need for one, yet according to the scriptures he enjoyed his fellowship with God.

> *Then the man and his wife heard the LORD God walking in the garden. It was the coolest time of the day. They hid from the Lord God among the trees of the garden.* (Genesis 1:8, NIV)

After the fall, Adam and Eve had two sons: Cain and Abel, who built altars and offered sacrifices to God as an act of worship. They too did not need a special title to offer sacrifices to God. Later on, God called Abraham and instructed him to leave his people and the city of Ur and move to a land God was going to show him. Abraham obeyed, and when he arrived the land of Canaan he built an altar and offered sacrifices to God. The LORD appeared to Abram at Shechem. He said, "I will give this land to your children after you." So Abram built an altar there to honor the Lord, who had appeared to him.

> *From there, Abram went on toward the hills east of Bethel. He set up his tent there. Bethel was to the*

> *west, and Ai was to the east. Abram built an altar*
> *there and worshiped the LORD.* (Genesis 12:7-8)

Later on, God changed Abraham's name from Abram to Abraham because he was going to become the father of many nations. This change of name represented a change in destiny, but was not accompanied by a lofty title. With time, Abraham's nephew, Lot, ran into trouble, so Abraham went to rescue him. After rescuing Lot, Abraham met Melchizedek, the King of Jerusalem, and a priest of God Most High.

> *Melchizedek was the king of Jerusalem. He brought*
> *out bread and wine. He was the priest of God Most*
> *High.* (Genesis 14:18)

This is the first time the Bible makes mention of a priest of God Most High. It's also intriguing to note that Melchizedek, who is a type of Christ, was also the King of Jerusalem. He appears suddenly in Scripture, and there has been speculation about who he is and where he came from. We are not going to address any of these issues. Melchizedek is mentioned here because he is the first priest mentioned in Scripture.

Isaac and Jacob did not have any special titles, but they served God faithfully. Jacob had 12 sons, who sold their brother Joseph to slave drivers. Joseph ended up in Egypt, and through him, Jacob and his entire family ended up in Egypt to escape a severe famine. With time, the children of Israel became slaves in Egypt and were treated harshly. Their cries for help and deliverance went up to God, so God sent Moses to deliver them from the hands of Pharaoh, King of Egypt. Moses had spent 40 years taking care of sheep, and God called him to go ask Pharaoh, king of the most powerful nation on earth, to let His people go. Even so, God did not confer on Moses any special title.

Moses is simply referred to as the servant of God and. In this context, it is a functional description of his obedience to God's instructions. Although Moses had no fancy title, he succeeded in delivering the children of Israel out of the bondage of Pharaoh through mighty and supernatural acts of God. In the desert, God asked the people to prepare themselves to meet Him, for God's intention was to make ALL the people into a nation of priests.

> *Now obey me completely. Keep my covenant. If you do, then out of all of the nations you will be my special treasure. The whole earth is mine. But you will be a kingdom of priests to serve me. You will be my holy nation. That is what you must tell the Israelites. So Moses went back. He sent for the elders of the people. He explained to them everything the LORD had commanded him to say. All of the people answered together. They said, 'We*

will do everything the LORD HAS SAID.' (Exodus 19:5-7)

The people said they would do everything Moses had instructed so that God's promise to make them into a nation of priests would be realized. Becoming a nation of priests was not an impossible task. We have already seen that their forefathers had all offered sacrifices to God and worshiped God without any intermediaries.

The long stay of the Israelites in Egypt might have influenced their understanding of who they were, and God was about to change all that. Unfortunately, the people did not follow through. They decided to tell Moses to represent them before God. Perhaps they thought it would take a lot of hard work to get ready to become a nation of priests; they would rather have Moses do it on their behalf.

> *The people saw the thunder and lightning. They heard the trumpet. They saw the mountain covered with smoke. They trembled with fear and stayed a long way off. They said to Moses, 'Speak to us yourself. Then we'll listen. But don't let God speak to us. If he does, we'll die.'* (Exodus 20:18-19)

According to the Scripture above, the Israelites would rather have Moses speak to them than have God speak to them directly. Fear kept them from God, and today the song remains the same, as fear is keeping Christians from approaching the throne of God.

God responded to the desire of the children of Israel and established the Levitical priesthood. Aaron was the first High Priest, while many other priests served under him in the tabernacle and eventually in the temple when they arrived in the Promised Land.

TITLES DURING THE TIME OF CHRIST

The Messiah, our Lord and Savior Jesus Christ, was born in a manger among sheep and cattle. One would have expected the Son of God to come in pomp and pageantry. That was not the case. This is an indication of how different God's ways are from those of man.

Jesus was referred to by many titles, and all these titles described who he was and testified to what he did. He declared that, 'I am the Light of the World, the Bread of Life, the Way, the Truth, and the Life, the Good Shepherd.' Some called Him Rabbi, Teacher, Master, and the Lamb of God who takes away the sins of the world. The Bible declares the following concerning Jesus Christ, '*In the beginning, the Word was already there. The Word was with God, and the Word was God. He was with God in the beginning. All things were made through him. Nothing that has been made was made without him.'* (John 1:1-3)

Jesus had every right to take upon himself any title, but He did not. Instead, He referred to Himself as the 'son of man' on many occasions, and discouraged others from taking on lofty titles. He had some strong words against the Pharisees and teachers of the law, and He cautioned his disciples from following their example of taking on titles:

> *But you shouldn't be called 'Rabbi.' You have only one Master, and you are all brothers. Do not call anyone on earth 'father.' You have one Father, and he is in heaven. You shouldn't be called 'teacher.' You have one Teacher, and he is the Christ. The most important person among you will be your servant. Anyone who lifts himself up will be brought down. And anyone who is brought down will be lifted up.* (Mathew 23:8-12)

Commenting on this passage, J.C. Ryle states:

Happy would it have been for the Church of Christ, if this passage had been more deeply pondered, and the spirit of it more implicitly obeyed. The Pharisees are not the only people who have imposed austerities on others, and affected the sanctity of apparel, and loved the praise of man. The annals of church history show that only too many Christians have walked closely in their steps. (Ryle's Expository Thoughts on the Gospels, Vol.1 [Grand Rapids: Baker Book House Reprint, 1977] p.299)

During Jesus' time on Earth, the Pharisees and teachers of the Law were those who were charged with teaching the law of God to others. They loved to sit in high places during occasions and insisted on being called Rabbi by the rest of the people. This is not different from some of the present day practices of our clergy. Titles have come to symbolize power and influence, the prerogative to sit at the high table with those that matter in each community. Should we not call this modern Pharisee-ism?

Jesus had other plans. That is why he chose fishermen and people that many dismissed as nobodies to be his first disciples. Before He left, He gave them these marching orders:

> *Then Jesus came to them. He said, 'All authority in heaven and on earth has been given to me. So you must go and make disciples of all nations. Baptize them in the name of the Father and of the Son and of the Holy Spirit. Teach them to obey everything I have commanded you. And you can be sure that I am always with you, to the very end.' (Mathew 28: 18-20)*

The instruction of Jesus is clear in this passage, but the church has willfully refused to follow it. The desire to get rid of the lording over people practiced by the Pharisees was at the heart of what Jesus said here. In objection to the positional use of titles by the church, Greg Ogden, himself a shepherd, states:

> I mourn for the church because we seem to display so many of the characteristics that Jesus said, 'Not so among you' (Mark 10:43). **Shameful arrogance and haughtiness have reached epidemic proportions among church leaders** . . . A direct implication of Jesus' servant stance was His obliteration of titles . . . We have refused to take Jesus' words at face value. Jesus' obvious intent was to remove any basis for 'lording it over' others by dispensing with titles that give people an elevated place in the 'pecking order.' We all occupy the same level ground at the foot of the one Teacher, Jesus Christ. We are not 'great ones' or 'lords' . . . Finally, do not accept the designation 'master' or 'leader.' No human can usurp the position of the head of the body, Christ. Our tendency seems always toward idolatry, to make someone larger than life. Never forget: Jesus alone is Lord. (The New Reformation: Returning the Ministry to

the People of God [Grand Rapids: Zondervan, 1990] p.172, 174)

TITLES IN THE EARLY CHURCH AND BEYOND

There is no record of titles being used in the New Testament. Paul referred to himself as Paul the apostle. The elders placed in charge of the churches Paul established were called brothers and sisters. There is no elder James, John, Peter etc. There is no teacher Andrew, or Evangelist Mark. All the brethren were addressed as saints of God. This is evident in the letters Paul wrote to the different churches. That is why the following verses in Ephesians have to be taken seriously if one wants to understand the root cause of the title pandemic in Christendom today:

He is the One who gave some the gift to be apostles. He gave some the gift to be prophets. He gave some the gift of preaching the good news. And he gave some the gift to be pastors and teachers. He did it so that they might prepare God's people to serve. If they do, the body of Christ will be built up. That will continue until we all become one in the faith and in the knowledge of God's Son. Then we will be grown up in the faith. We will receive everything that Christ has for us. We will no longer be babies in the faith. We won't be like ships tossed around by the waves. We won't be blown here and there by every new teaching. We won't be blown around by the cleverness and tricks of people who try to hide their evil plans. [15] Instead, we will speak the truth in love. We will grow up into Christ in every way. He is the Head. He makes the whole body grow and build itself up in love. Under the control of Christ, each part of the body does its work. It supports the other parts. In that way, the body is joined and held together. (Ephesians 4:11-16)

The use and misuse, as well as the abuses and excesses associated with titles in Christendom are rooted in an improper interpretation of this part of Scripture. The giver of the gifts has one purpose, and that is to ensure that the recipients of these gifts participate in the spiritual growth and development of their brethren, with the ultimate goal being spiritual maturity. Mature adults do what adults do, and there is no exception in the ministry. That is why the first part of these verses of scripture state that, "The saints are to be equipped for the work of the ministry." In other words, the saints are called to be ministers.

From all indications, the early church was not driven by titles. Unfortunately, the conversion of Emperor Constantine in 312 AD to Christianity resulted in the

24

marriage between the church and State. All of a sudden the Christian church that was often persecuted and at the fringe of society became a State church. Everybody was expected to become a Christian, and Christian Leaders adopted the world's power hierarchies that had been previously alien to the church.

This new marriage over the years led to excesses and abuse of functional roles in the church, and in the 14th century, Martin Luther attempted to reform the system. That reformation, however, was not completed. Therefore, there is a call today for a second reformation, where the priesthood of the saints is returned to the saints and the unbiblical division between "clergy" and "laity" is abolished. This will get rid of all the superfluous titles being used in Christendom today.

CHAPTER 3

PROPHETS, APOSTLES, AND BISHOPS: A BIBLICAL PERSPECTIVE

The use of titles has become a widespread practice in the Christian faith today. Titles affect social power relations and feed the human desire for social recognition. However, it is an empty drum when self-bestowed without corresponding achievements to go with it. If an individual announces that he or she is a 'mechanical

Emmanuel Nuesiri

engineer' and begins using the title 'engineer,' people assume that person has obtained a proper degree in engineering and passed all the required professional

27

exams. If indeed the individual has done this, then he or she can rightfully expect the salary and privileges associated with being a qualified engineer. So, titles do not just feed the human desire for social recognition, but have implications on the type and magnitude of power resources accessible to us. A married person can lay exclusive claim to the romantic embrace of his or her spouse; a Pastor of an independent Church can expect to be in charge of the tithes paid by the Church members every month; a Bishop would expect the high chair in any Christian gathering; and an Apostle would expect no less recognition accorded to a Bishop, if not more.

Titles then are not neutral – they have an impact on the bearers and on the target group that recognizes such titles. It is this reality that ensures that professional titles are not easily granted by professional associations. In order to hold the title of a 'chartered accountant' recognized by the London Society of Chartered Accountants, the bearer would have studied many years and passed many qualifying exams. The scrutiny does not stop there. As a member of the London Society, the title bearer would be expected to practice his or her profession guided by a code of ethics to ensure that the bearer would not abuse the trust of his or her clients. Is this the same with title bearers in the Christian faith? How are titles awarded and how are title-bearers held accountable in the Christian faith?

Obviously, the many denominations in Christianity have a great number of ways and means of their adherents acquiring recognized titles, and would have different mechanisms to hold title-bearers accountable. Be this as it may, all Christian groups profess that the Bible guides them. So to the Bible we must turn to understand the basics of the use of titles by Christians and mechanisms of accountability for title-holders.

TITLES IN THE BIBLE

It is not possible to consider every title in the Bible; rather we will consider the title of 'Prophet' in the Old Testament, and the titles of 'Apostle' and 'Bishop' in the New Testament. The objective is to show how the title is acquired and the accountability mechanisms behind these titles. The goal is to draw lessons from these that would be helpful to us today. All scriptural quotations are from the King James Bible except when specified otherwise. It should be stated that the discussions below take for granted that the five-fold ministry of Ephesians 4 and the gifts of the Holy Spirit in 1 Corinthians 12 are still operational in the Church today. They are for establishing the foundations of the Church (Ephesians 2:20) and are also for the building up of the Church until we all attain the fullness of the maturity of Christ (Ephesians 4:12-14). We have the complete canon of scripture, but we are not yet the bride of Christ without spots or wrinkles (Ephesians 5:27), so we do need the five-fold ministries and the Holy Spirit to get us there.

The 'Prophet' of the Old Testament

The Prophets were the preachers in Old Testament Israel. How did an Israelite become a Prophet? The case of Samuel is instructive in this regard, as reported in 1 Samuel Chapter 3; let's consider the narrative from verses 8 to 10:

> *And the Lord called Samuel again the third time. And he arose and went to Eli, and said, here am I; for thou didst call me. And Eli perceived that the Lord had called the child. Therefore Eli said unto Samuel, Go, lie down: and it shall be, if he call thee, that thou shalt say, Speak, Lord; for thy servant heareth. So Samuel went and lay down in his place. And the Lord came, and stood, and called as at other times, Samuel, Samuel. Then Samuel answered, Speak; for thy servant heareth.*

Samuel was called by God three times but did not understand what was happening. Eli had to advise him to answer the voice calling him. It still took a while before he responded, as the passage above shows. Samuel became one of Israel's great prophets, as the

Bible records that God did not let any of his words fall to the ground (1 Sam. 3:19).

A close look at the life of Samuel reveals that he concerned himself with judging the people, as in solving disputes that normally arise in any society, and with the national issues of concern to the people. He anointed Saul for the kingship, and later did the same with David. He guided Saul on how to handle the wars with Israel's enemies and scolded Saul the king when necessary. Prophets in Israel were called by God not just to minister to the individual problems the people brought to them, but were intimately involved with the government and governance of Israel. This is true of Moses, Samuel, Elijah, Isaiah, and all of the Old Testament Prophets. Is this the same for prophets in the New Testament? Let's consider the Prophet Agabus[1], mentioned twice in the Bible. The first instance is in Acts 11:27-28:

> *And in these days came prophets from Jerusalem unto Antioch. And there stood up one of them named Agabus, and signified by the Spirit that there should be great dearth throughout all the*

---

[1] In this section we are concerned with the ministry or office of the prophet, and not with the gift of prophecy (1 Corinthians 12) which is available to every Christian filled with the Holy Spirit

world: which came to pass in the days of Claudius Caesar.

Agabus prophesied that there would be worldwide famine. The next verses show that his message stirred the believers in Antioch who were economically better off than the brethren in Jerusalem to send help to those in Jerusalem. His message to the Church enabled the Church to take appropriate steps to help those who were in desperate need. This prophecy, as we see here, is closely tied to the government and governance of God's Church. The second instance when Agabus is mentioned is in Acts 21:10-11:

And as we tarried there many days, there came down from Judaea a certain prophet, named Agabus. And when he was come unto us, he took Paul's girdle, and bound his own hands and feet, and said, Thus saith the Holy Ghost, So shall the Jews at Jerusalem bind the man that owneth this girdle, and shall deliver him into the hands of the Gentiles.

Earlier in Acts 21, the Church in the city of Tyre had warned Paul through a prophecy not to travel to Jerusalem. Paul and those travelling with him did not react to this warning until Agabus met them at Caesarea and spoke clearly of what would happen to

Paul in Jerusalem. The prophecy troubled the Church; many wept fearing for Paul's safety.

We see from these two narratives that the prophecies of Agabus to the Church spoke to events that would have a major impact on the Church. This is not to say Agabus would not have had time for individuals to come to him with their personal problems. Scripture shows clearly in the Old and New Testament that prophets are a source of comfort to many during times of troubles. However, we are not short of individuals who address personal struggles in people's lives today. People who end up calling themselves prophets but totally ignore and neglect the fact that prophets are also called to address issues important to the corporate Church. Indeed, the ministry of the prophet goes beyond the personal to matters with heavy consequences for the Church.

The question then is how do people who claim to be prophets in Churches today compare to the Agabus standard? Where are the prophets speaking to matters that concern the Church in Cameroon, the Church across Africa, and the Church all over the world? Has God stopped sending the Church such individuals? How do we hold prophets accountable for the messages they deliver? There are several passages in the Old Testament to help us. The first is Deuteronomy 18:22:

When a prophet speaketh in the name of the Lord, if the thing follow not, nor come to pass, that is the thing which the Lord hath not spoken, but the prophet hath spoken it presumptuously: thou shalt not be afraid of him.

And the other is Jeremiah 28:9: *The prophet which prophesieth of peace, when the word of the prophet shall come to pass, then shall the prophet be known, that the Lord hath truly sent him.*

And there is also Ezekiel 33:33: *And when this cometh to pass, (lo, it will come,) then shall they know that a prophet hath been among them.*

What do these verses have in common? They all refer to situations where the prophet is giving a prophecy to the nation of Israel, and not when the prophet is dealing with individual problems. So the prophet is assessed on whether the messages he (or she) delivers to Israel eventually comes to pass. Does this mean that if a person who claims to be a prophet predicts that a particular nation will win the football (soccer) World Cup and it happens that person is a prophet from God? No, this is not proof that the individual is God's prophet.

There are spiritualists and occultists who can perfectly predict such things. The place where God's prophets of today are different is their ability to prophesy about issues that have a direct impact on the Church. The great popularity of prophets today whose prophecies start and end with private issues that Church members are passing through indicates a scarcity of vision concerning the bigger problems facing the Church today. A minister who saw clearly through the problems facing the Church today and left us great wisdom on how to live victoriously in an age of compromise was Aiden Wilson Tozer (1897-1963). A. W. Tozer, as he is commonly known, is considered a prophet to the modern Church. His book, '*Reclaiming Christianity: A Call to Authentic Faith,*' is a must read prophetic work for everyone who desires to know God's mind about the Church today.[2] Let's now turn our attention to the titles of 'Apostle' and 'Bishop' in the New Testament Church.

The 'Apostle' of the New Testament

The title 'Apostle' is widely understood in the Church today to mean 'messenger' sent out to proclaim the gospel and plant Churches. In the New Testament, it is first used to refer to the 12 individuals who Jesus called to come and work with him to proclaim the gospel of the kingdom. Paul later referred to himself as an Apostle in Ephesians 1:1. Paul goes on to show in Ephesians that the Church has received five ministerial gifts from

---

2   The introduction and Chapter 1 of this book are available online at http://www.tozeraw.com/wp-content/uploads/2013/09/reclaiming-christianity-sample.pdf

the Lord to be used in the perfecting of the saints. Ephesians 4:11-12 says:

And he gave some, apostles; and some, prophets; and some, evangelists; and some, pastors and teachers; for the perfecting of the saints, for the work of the ministry, for the edifying of the body of Christ:

So the honor of being an apostle is not self-given; it is a gift from God. What are the credentials of an apostle? The apostles in the book of Acts were pioneers taking the gospel to unreached people and unreached nations. This was accompanied by a great deal of suffering and self-sacrifice, as is the case with pioneering efforts in any field of human achievement. The sufferings of the apostles were extraordinary because Satan was determined to crush them and halt the spread of the gospel. The extraordinary sacrifice of the apostles partly explains why Paul writes in Ephesians 2:19-20 that:

Now therefore ye are no more strangers and foreigners, but fellow citizens with the saints, and of the household of God; And are built upon the foundation of the apostles and prophets, Jesus Christ himself being the chief corner stone;

Paul is stating clearly that we the Church 'are built upon the foundation of the apostles and prophets.' The greater the house being built, the deeper, the stronger the foundation has to be in order to carry the load and pressure of the house without it collapsing. The lesson here is that the apostolic ministry is for the mature, self-sacrificing minister. Apostles as pioneers, stepping into the unknown and reaching groups that were hitherto unreached by the gospel message, are at the forefront of the war between heaven and hell. Apostleship is a heavy-duty title, not to be taken lightly. How can the Church hold accountable persons who take on the title 'Apostle?' Let's consider Acts 17:10-11:

And the brethren immediately sent away Paul and Silas by night unto Berea: who coming thither went into the synagogue of the Jews. These were nobler than those in Thessalonica, in that they received the word with all readiness of mind, and searched the scriptures daily, whether those things were so.

Christians have to test the teachings of an apostle through diligent Bible study to verify or refuse the teachings and mentorship of such individuals. In addition to being self-sacrificing pioneers, persons who cannot rightly handle the Bible cannot be apostles.

In Cameroon, we have had outstanding ministers like the late Zach Tanee Fomum, founder of the Christian Missionary Fellowship International (CMFI), and Weiner Knorr, founder of the Full Gospel Mission Cameroon (FGMC), who qualify as Apostles to

Cameroon. Others like Nigerian William F. Kumuyi and American T. L. Osborn, who recently passed away, are also without a doubt modern-day Apostles.

Today, many young converts quickly affix 'Apostle' to their names after planting one or two Churches, instead of allowing the body of believers to observe their track record and accord them the respect due apostles; they quickly jump the gun and seize the title 'Apostle' for themselves. These people lack humility, demand slave-like service from brethren in their flock, and preach money at every opportunity they get – proving that their God is their belly, as Paul writes in Philippians 3:17-19:

> *Brethren, be followers together of me, and mark them which walk so as ye have us for an ensample. For many walk, of whom I have told you often, and now tell you even weeping, that they are the enemies of the cross of Christ: Whose end is destruction, whose God is their belly, and whose glory is in their shame, who mind earthly things.*

Who is an apostle and how can we know them? Paul's answer, following his instruction in the above verses, would be those whose lives follow the examples set by the lives of the apostles in the Bible. The apostolic calling is one that involves deep self-sacrifice for the Lord and the advancement of the gospel; it is not about personal glory, as some seem to think today.

The 'Bishop' of the New Testament

The office of 'Bishop' is extremely popular today and now includes the rank 'Archbishop,' denoting a senior bishop who presides over other bishops. Both Paul and Peter mention the office of bishop in a number of New Testament passages. Let us consider what Paul says about the office of bishop in 1 Timothy 3:1-6:

> *This is a true saying, If a man desire the office of a bishop, he desireth a good work. A bishop then must be blameless, the husband of one wife, vigilant, sober, of good behaviour, given to hospitality, apt to teach; Not given to wine, no striker, not greedy of filthy lucre; but patient, not a brawler, not covetous; One that ruleth well his own house, having his children in subjection with all gravity;* **(For if a man know not how to rule his own house, how shall he take care of the church of God?)** *Not a novice, lest being lifted up with pride he fall into the condemnation of the devil.*

In the above quoted passage, Paul is instructing Timothy about factors to consider before appointing men into the position of bishops, men who would be expected to '*take care of the church of God.*' Paul gives similar instructions in Titus 1:5-9:

> For this cause left I thee in Crete, that thou shouldest set in order the things that are wanting, and **ordain elders in every city**, as I had appointed thee: If any be blameless, the husband of one wife, having faithful children not accused of riot or unruly. **For a bishop must be blameless**, as the steward of God; not selfwilled, not soon angry, not given to wine, no striker, not given to filthy lucre; But a lover of hospitality, a lover of good men, sober, just, holy, temperate; Holding fast the faithful word as he hath been taught, that he may be able by sound doctrine both to exhort and to convince the gainsayers.

In this passage we can see that Paul considers the office of 'elder' as one and the same with the office of 'bishop.' Timothy and Titus were to appoint experienced men to care for the many local Churches in their mission field. These would be married men with a source of income to care for their families who would also be full of wisdom, as evidenced in the behavior of their children. They were also to be men who were 'apt to teach,' or, as Paul said in 1Timothy 5:17, men who 'labour in the word and doctrine.'

By the standards and practice of today, Timothy and Titus would be 'Archbishops,' and Paul, who mentored both men, would be the 'Pope' or possibly 'Super Papa Apostle Archbishop Paul.' The bishops, or elders, ordained by Timothy and Titus were quite obviously helpers caring for various Churches in the mission field presided over by Timothy and Titus. The tradition today, with bishops and archbishops in kingly robes with crowns, in which the office of bishop is sometimes elevated above the five-fold ministry (see Ephesians 4), is not supported by Paul's teachings in scripture. In 1 Peter 2:24-25, Peter says this:

> *Who his own self- bare our sins in his own body on the tree, that we, being dead to sins, should live unto righteousness: by whose stripes ye were healed. For ye were as sheep going astray; but are now returned unto the Shepherd and Bishop of your souls.*

While Peter is here teaching about Jesus, conjoining 'Shepherd <u>and</u> Bishop' in the passage, he is showing that bishops are shepherds, that is, sacrificial pastoral care providers. This is opposite to traditions of today, where bishops act like kings over God's flock (or queens where women are ordained as bishops). This kingly behavior is evident from what they wear, their manner of speech, and how they interact with 'ordinary' Church

41

members. It seems we have not heeded Paul's warning in the way we appoint bishops, so we have ended up with many 'being lifted up with pride' (1 Timothy 3:6). Indeed, If Paul considered the office of Bishop, which Paul also referred to as 'elder,' a royal, elevated office, how could he have imagined the bishop being subject to the discipline of the church, as we read in 1 Timothy 5:19, 20 – "Against an elder receive not an accusation, but before two or three witnesses. Them that sin rebuke before all, that others also may fear."

CONCLUSION

How should we then understand the use of titles in Scripture following from the case studies of 'Prophets,' 'Apostles,' and 'Bishops' that this Chapter has examined? Firstly, these titles are linked to the functions of these individuals in God's household, be it Israel in the Old Testament or the Church in the New Testament. Secondly, scriptural titles are different from titles linked to salaried professionals, like 'principal' of a school, or 'director' of a company. These professional titles are linked to the provision of services to society that people pay for. The principal manages a school that provides educational services that we pay for. The director manages a company that produces a product, perhaps shoes that we pay to obtain. Out of our payments, the principal or the director receives a salary. Scriptural titles are not linked to products; they are linked to the spiritual work of building God's people up in knowledge and character until we attain the full stature of Jesus Christ.

It is therefore a bit worrying when some leaders of ministries prefer to be known as 'chief executive officers' (CEO)[3]. This is from the business world, where the visionary purpose at the end of the day is to make money. Business principles cannot be the same principles as in God's kingdom. Thirdly, titles in scriptures are self-sacrificial lifetime callings from which there is no retirement. As ministers get older, they do slowdown in their day-to-day physical activities, but not in their seeking of God in the place of prayer and Bible study. Title holders in the Church never get to a place where God settles you, and all you have to do is sit on a nice comfortable big chair, eating, drinking, and sleeping after a job well done. God's principle is to start us with a little responsibility, and if we are faithful, to gradually increase it. Following this principle, a young or immature Christian cannot humbly function

---

3   The well-respected Bible teacher John Piper has a great book titled 'Brothers, We Are Not Professionals: A Plea to Pastors for Radical Ministry,' that addresses this in detail; the book encourages ministers to return back to depending on the Holy Spirit rather than copy the ways of professional sales-men out there in the world. A free copy of the book is here http://www.desiringgod.org/books/brothers-we-are-not-pro-fessionals

as prophet, apostle or bishop; these are strong meat callings, and we know what the scripture says about strong meat in Hebrews 5:14:

> *But strong meat belongeth to them that are of full age, even those who by reason of use have their senses exercised to discern both good and evil.*

We should not be quick to seek or confer titles or offices in the Church, and we should do so even more cautiously when it comes to the "strong meat" positions of prophet, apostle, and bishop. We should allow our faithfulness in ministry speak for us.

CHAPTER 4

SHOULD CHRISTIAN LEADERS ACQUIRE TITLES?

Here in the USA, I have interacted with people at different levels in the academia. I have worked with Assistant Professors, Professors, and with one Distinguished Professor (my PhD supervisor). Honestly, as I interacted with these scholars, I could tell the difference in their academic potential, and this led me to the conclusion

Patrick Tamukong

that there are hardly any "empty titles" in academics, at least in this part of the world. By "empty titles," I am referring to unmerited titles picked from the gutter, so to speak. Conversely, recent years have seen the proliferation of "empty titles" within Christianity. This proliferation is indicative of the spiritual decay or apostasy that our Lord Jesus Christ predicted would characterize the END TIMES. The Holy Spirit also speaking through Paul predicted that men should be lovers of themselves and lovers of pleasure rather than lovers of God (2 Timothy 3:1-4). The desire for recognition; the honor and prestige that surround titles is the impetus for the present mad rush for titles among most Christian leaders who have deviated from the "ancient path" of humility marked by Jesus Christ and His Apostles.

It is common nowadays in Christianity for people to pay money to obtain any certificate for which they never labored or underwent the required training. The discipline that accompanies the labor involved to acquire genuine titles indicates to society that the person with the title can be trusted with responsibilities that impact society. Contrarily, in some of today's Bible colleges, the curriculum is so scanty that when one looks at it, one wonders if the required course of study could possibly justify the "big" degrees or certificates handed out. In our Christian seminaries and Bible training institutes, it has become commonplace to complete Masters and PhD programs within six months (a rarity in secular institutions). Modern day Christians have grown increasingly lazy towards their faith, while at the same time loving the praises of men and earning such praises cheaply.

Coming to the question on whether Christian leaders are to seek after titles, it is important to remember the admonition in Hebrews 5:4 (NKJV) *"And no man takes this honor to himself, but he who is called by God, just as Aaron was."* To *acquire* is to *obtain, achieve, grab, gain, procure*, or to *lay hold of* something. This carries the sense of "running after" or "employing human energy or effort" in order to lay hold of something. This is the natural course of life. Humans are on speed to achieve one thing or another that will give them respect before others. Humans seek academic degrees not just for better jobs, but also for the honor that comes with such degrees. The race in academics seems endless. For several scholars, once they acquire the highest degree, such as doctor of philosophy (PhD), next comes the struggle for promotion to higher academic ranks. Simply put, the world is in competition with itself: students in competition with their colleagues, schools in competition with other schools, businesses in various markets, and even whole nations in competition with each other. Through these competing efforts, successful individuals, organizations, and nations attain certain positions or levels of admiration and recognition. Such recognition could be referred to as *titles*.

A *title* denotes an *appellation, inscription,* or *description* of one's position or function. Genuine titles are those conferred by a legitimate authority on a person or institution that has been tested and deemed qualified to receive such an honor. Some nations want to earn the title of the most economically powerful, others desire the title of the most militarily powerful, others aspire the title of the nation with the best educational system, and the list goes on. Businesses put in millions of dollars in advertisement not just for better sales, but also because they are in a cold war with competitors.

Whereas in the system of this world, people toil to secure positions, honor and the profit that goes with it, the Principles of God's Kingdom run contrary. God's Kingdom Principles are in opposition to those of this present fallen world that is fading away *"...for what is highly esteemed among men is an abomination in the sight of God,"* (Luke 16:15, NKJV). God tends to put LAST that which the world puts FIRST; honor in God's Kingdom comes through servant leadership. This is *"because the foolishness of God is wiser than men; and the weakness of God is stronger than men"* (1 Corinthians 1:25, NKJV). Moreover, in His Wisdom, God has chosen foolish things to confound the wise, and weak things to confound the strong, so that no flesh may glory before Him (1 Corinthians 1:27-29).

Jesus chose simple people to be His disciples. It is a principle of God's Kingdom that "no flesh should glory in His presence." In fact, two of Jesus' closest associates, Peter and John, were regarded by the religious leaders of their day as "uneducated and untrained men" (Acts

4:13). Those God calls to Himself must necessarily strip themselves of honors according to the world's standards and take up the yoke of Christ to learn of His meekness and humility daily (Matthew 11:29-30). This is "denial of the SELF" emphasized at different points in the Bible as a prerequisite for discipleship. Whoever in CHRIST thinks him/herself to be wise by the standards of this world is thus exhorted to become foolish in order to truly get wise by learning from the Holy Spirit (1 Corinthians 3:18).

THE GIFT OF GOD

And He Himself gave some to be apostles, some prophets, some evangelists, and some pastors and teachers, for the equipping of the saints for the work of ministry, for the edifying of the body of Christ (Ephesians 4:11-12, NKJV).

Christian ministry is the Gift of God. It is not anything comparable to what is offered in the secular world. It cannot be earned by self-effort. No amount of study can earn one a ministry in God's Kingdom. No one takes upon himself the honor of entering a ministry office. It is reserved solely for those whom the Lord has called, and no one can decide to work his/her way into it. Whereas those the Lord has called are exhorted to study to be effective (2 Timothy 2:15), no one could presume to attain a spiritual office by study. If it (Christian ministry and, as a result, a title) can be *acquired*, then it ceases to be a *gift*. One could admire and desire a position in the Church, such as the office of an Elder or Bishop (1 Timothy 3:1), but one must wait on God's call. Ambition for positions in God's Kingdom is a disease that manifested even among Jesus' disciples. Matthew 20:20-28 records the account of the sons of Zebedee who came (with their mother) worshipping Jesus and desiring to be placed at the highest positions in His Kingdom. Many people come to Jesus worshipping Him, but with the wrong motives. In verse 22 of Matthew chapter 20, Jesus apparently gave them the condition for achieving their end, which was "to drink the cup and to be baptized with the baptism of His sufferings." Although these "honor-hungry" brethren quickly responded in the affirmative, Jesus told them that they could not attain such positions, even after drinking the cup and being baptized with His baptism of sufferings:

> *So He said to them, 'You will indeed drink My cup, and be baptized with the baptism that I am baptized with; but to sit on My right hand and on My left is not Mine to give, but it is for those for whom it is prepared by My Father.'* (Matthew 20:23, NKJV)

This verse underscores, once again, that positions in God's Kingdom are for those called by God; that is, those for whom it is prepared by the Father. Although Ephesians 4:11-12 tells us that Jesus gave gifts, it is the Father who orchestrates all things in the Kingdom. The Father initiates all things and the Son administrates all things, while the Holy Spirit effects or carries out the desires of the Godhead. I have heard people teach about spiritual gifts and state that the Father, the Son, and the Holy Spirit have each given gifts to the Church. That is incorrect. The Father, Son, and Holy Spirit are one and inseparable. Any teaching that appears to divide them is incongruent with Biblical Truth. The Father initiates all things in the Kingdom, the Son administrates, while the Holy Spirit carries out the desires of the Godhead. It takes the Holy Spirit to carry out any work in God's Kingdom acceptably.

Christian ministry is God's Gift, and it is not an exaggeration to state that God generally calls those who are not anxious or desire getting into those offices. A key trait of a Divine Vision and/ or Responsibility is that it is overwhelming when it comes to a human being and such a person will need God's encouragement in order to accept the call and step out in obedience to God. Examples of such encouragement from God are seen in the cases of Moses (Exodus 3:12), Jeremiah (Jeremiah 1:7), and Ezekiel (Ezekiel 3:8-9).

PHARISAIC ATTITUDES IN THE BODY OF CHRIST TODAY

But all their works they do to be seen by men. They make their phylacteries broad and enlarge the borders of their garments. They love the best places at feasts, the best seats in the synagogues, greetings in the marketplaces, and to be called by men, 'Rabbi, Rabbi.' But you, do not be called 'Rabbi'; for One is your Teacher, the Christ, and you are all brethren. Do not call anyone on earth your father; for One is your Father, He who is in heaven. And do not be called teachers; for One is your Teacher, the Christ. But he who is greatest among you shall be your servant. And whoever exalts himself will be humbled, and he who humbles himself will be exalted (Matthew 23:5-12, NKJV).

In the above passage, Jesus warned His followers of the yeast of the Pharisees, which was their hypocrisy, and their craving for worldly honor, reflected in their desire to be treated with respect. The Pharisees would wear garments with broad phylacteries and enlarged borders in order to command respect from the people of their day; to be greeted with reverence and assigned to chief seats in the Church. Such regalia, however, did not characterize the lives of the Disciples of Christ. Jesus and His disciples often dressed simply such that the soldiers who came to arrest Jesus to be crucified could not distinguish Him from His disciples on the basis of how they were dressed. The traitor had to kiss Jesus in order for the assailants to identify and pick Him (Mark 14:44).

The spirit of the Pharisees is quite evident in the Church today. One would find ministers of the Gospel arrayed in ecclesiastical robes and collars. The world has designed robes, collars, and phylacteries for ministers in some Christian denominations, and this practice seems to be spreading. Hidden behind such regalia is not a passion for spiritual ministry but a desire to be respected by the people. Bluntly put, behind such externalities is the spirit of the Pharisees; the same motivation that was in the Pharisees, against which Jesus warned His disciples. He told his disciples not to aspire for titles such as "teacher" or "rabbi," or "master." Although He knew that Peter would later lead the rest of the Disciples, He gave Peter no special title, but rather referred to ALL of them as "brethren." After His departure, we never find Peter assuming any special title that placed Him above his brethren serving together as Apostles. In today's society, Peter would have been named "Chief Apostle" or "Arch Bishop." Although the titles "Bishop" and "Elder" mean the same thing, the former variant has become popular nowadays.

Behind such popularity is not a desire to sincerely serve as an Elder in God's Church, but rather, the spirit of the Pharisees: the desire to be recognized and revered by the world as "general overseer," "senior pastor," or "founder." Externality is typical of the Pharisees, whom Jesus compared to whitewashed tombs (Matthew 23:27). Jesus said the Pharisees did all their works to be seen by men. They were men-pleasers seeking earthly and not heavenly approval. Thus, they craved titles because they believed that was what would open doors for recognition and honor. The same selfish spirit rules many people supposedly serving Jesus today. One would hear them defend their actions by stating that they go for titles because titles open doors for them. Of course, that is the wrong motivation for ministry, a selfish craving for opened doors to satisfy one's lusts. As a good rule of thumb, if God has called you to serve in His Vineyard, do not try to open any door by self-effort that God has not opened to you.

THE SPIRIT OF SIMON IN THE BODY OF CHRIST TODAY

And when Simon saw that through the laying on of the apostles' hands the Holy Spirit was given, he offered them money, saying, "Give me this power also, that anyone on whom I lay hands may receive the Holy Spirit." But Peter said to him, "Your money perish with you, because you thought that the gift of God could be purchased with money! You have neither part nor portion in this matter, for your heart is not right in the sight of God. Repent therefore of this your wickedness, and pray God if perhaps the thought of your heart may be forgiven you. For I see that you are poisoned by bitterness and bound by iniquity." (Acts 8:18-23, NKJV).

The striving for titles common in Christian circles today is the pursuit of power and influence over people. This was the same lust in the heart of Simon, the sorcerer in the above passage. He had enjoyed popularity gained through his display of satanic anointing in Samaria prior to the coming of Philip, who was full of the Holy Spirit and who performed many superior miracles. Having lost his popularity, Simon had "believed" Philip's message because of the miracles he had seen and not because he had encountered Jesus as Savior. Thus, Simon was yet in the gall of bitterness and in the bond of iniquity, though a Church member. He was persuaded that the power of the Holy Spirit was superior to the satanic power he had, and offered Peter money in exchange for the anointing of the Holy Spirit.

Several of the calibers of Gospel ministers I see around me nowadays would have gladly accepted

Simon's money as a seed into the ministry. Peter, however, was different because he had truly been with Jesus. The sharp rebuke from Peter appears to have benefited Simon, who demanded mercy and prayers for his life (Acts 8:24).

There are many Simons today who deserve a sharp rebuke, but unfortunately, very few Peters are there to correct them. On one end, there are people today ready to pay money to achieve an ecclesiastical title and ordination. In fact, some Christian ministers have obtained their titles this way. On the other end, there are also people today who demand money for ordinations and who demand money in exchange for the anointing of God. You would hear such folks tell you to sow a seed for your miracle, sow a seed in order to connect to the grace, and so on. There are places one could simply pay money and have them offer him/her a doctorate or ordain him/her a "Bishop," "Bishop Doctor," "Apostle," "Prophet," and the list continues.

This buying and selling of God's 'grace' and titles is contrary to Biblical Truth. Truly called servants of God do not cling to titles and will not run for them to the extent of offering money to get them. The world was more focused on assigning a title to John the Baptist, the forerunner of our Lord Jesus Christ, but we see from John's response that he was more focused on the mission God had called him to fulfill as a voice of one crying in the wilderness. Such is the spirit of those truly called of God.

> *Now this is the testimony of John, when the Jews sent priests and Levites from Jerusalem to ask him, "Who are you?" He confessed, and did not deny, but confessed, "I am not the Christ." And they asked him, "What then? Are you Elijah?" He said, "I am not." "Are you the Prophet?" And he answered, "No." Then they said to him, "Who are you, that we may give an answer to those who sent us? What do you say about yourself?" He said: "I am 'The voice of one crying in the wilderness: "Make straight the way of the Lord,"' as the prophet Isaiah said." Now those who were sent were from the Pharisees* (John 1:19-24, NKJV).

Although Jesus stated that none greater than John the Baptist had ever risen (Matt. 11:11), John the Baptist did not assume a title. The Pharisees became troubled when they found such an anointed and influential man without any title. Hence, they sent people to seek John's identity. John's response left them confused. Genuine men of God in contemporary times have had to resist pressure from the world seeking to force titles down their throats. The attitude seen in John the Baptist was likewise in Moses. Although God had made him a god to Pharaoh with Aaron as his prophet (Exodus 7:1), he remained known simply as Moses. At no time in his ministry did he become "god Moses." The people would refer to him as *"...this Moses..."* (Exodus 32:1, NKJV). Moses is perhaps one of the greatest servants of God in the Scriptures; one who spoke with God face to face. Yet Moses is not seen clinging to any special title. Such is the attitude of genuine ministers of God. The Lord Jesus Christ is our example of excellence. As Son of man, He taught His followers not to desire empty worldly honor. He rebuked religious Jews in the following words:

> *I do not receive honor from men. But I know you, that you do not have the love of God in you. I have come in My Father's name, and you do not receive Me; if another comes in his own name, him you will receive. How can you believe, who receive honor from one another, and do not seek the honor that comes from the only God?* (John 5:41-44, NKJV).

Jesus' honor didn't come from this world, and neither should ours. He didn't seek big titles while on the earth because He didn't need worldly recognition and acceptance, and neither do we. The words of our Master, Jesus Christ, in the above citation suggest that people who seek worldly honor have a heart problem; they lack the love of God, and the result is spiritual blindness. Such folks would gladly receive people who come to them **"in their own names"** but not those who come "**in the name of the Lord.**" Gospel ministers who cling to titles and worldly regalia go to the people in their own names. When they come to a city, they come in the name of the Apostle, the Prophet, the Bishop, and so on. Folks with a heart problem embrace such ministers who come in their own names. On the other hand, genuine ministers of the Gospel, who have lost their identity in the Lord Jesus Christ, who are dead and have had their lives become hidden with Christ in God (Colossians 3:3), can only come in the name of the Lord. Such have nothing to boast about and nothing to brandish before their listeners to show their self-importance. Jesus came in the name of His Father and the world rejected Him. Jesus' identity was lost in His Father and He would repeatedly state "*...Most assuredly, I say to you, the Son can do nothing of Himself, but what He sees the Father do; for whatever He does, the Son also does in like manner*" (John 5:19, NKJV). The world repels those who come in the name of the Lord, but embraces and makes friends with those who come in their own names.

Genuine ministers of the Gospel are not man made, nor are they pleasers of men. Paul introduced himself to the Galatians in the following words, "*Paul, an apostle, (not of men, neither by man, but by Jesus Christ, and God the Father, who raised him from the dead,*" (Galatians 1:1, KJV). Paul was not an Apostle **of men**. In other words, Paul didn't seek to please men in his presentation of the

Gospel. There are many Apostles **of men** nowadays who speak enticing words full of human wisdom to please their listeners.

Secondly, Paul was not an Apostle **by man**. In other words, the Lord Jesus Christ and the Father made him an Apostle, not mortal men. Nowadays, one finds people purportedly serving our Lord Jesus Christ by inviting others to crown them with titles and ecclesiastical regalia. Such seek the honor that comes from this world and are not serving our Master Jesus Christ in truth. Their god is their belly and their glory is in their shame, according to Philippians 3. They are Apostles/Bishops/Prophets/Honorary Doctors of men and by man. The Lord didn't send them, yet they went in His name and acquired titles.

DO YOU SEEK TITLES FOR YOURSELF?

We have shown in this chapter that Christian leaders should not acquire ecclesiastical titles. Does this suggest that the use of titles is unbiblical? No. Titles exist in the Scriptures, but true servants of the Lord do not make a show of them. True servants of God do not live in the consciousness of titles and would introduce themselves without emphasizing their titles. For example, James, the brother of Jesus, referred to himself simply as *"...a bondservant of God..."* (James 1:1, NKJV) while John referred to himself as *"The Elder..."* (2 John 1:1; 3 John 1:1, NKJV). Bible authors who introduced themselves with a ministerial title included would generally write their first names before the titles. In that way, they emphasized their names over their titles. Those who brandish titles for self-importance would place the title before their names, and some folks nowadays would place multiple titles before their names.

To address a genuine minister of the Gospel by the corresponding biblical title (Prophet, Teacher, or Evangelist) is not wrong. By "genuine minister," I am referring to those called, equipped, and accredited by the Lord. When the Lord calls, He prepares and introduces:

> *Behold! My Servant whom I uphold, My Elect One in whom My soul delights! I have put My Spirit upon Him; He will bring forth justice to the Gentiles* (Isaiah 42:1, NKJV).

And then He accredits:

> *Fellow Israelites, listen to this: Jesus of Nazareth was a man accredited by God to you by miracles, wonders and signs, which God did among you through him, as you yourselves know.* (Acts 2:22, NIV)

As we discuss the use of titles in Christianity, let us remember that the greatest title for any follower of Jesus is *Servant*. Whether one is called to be an Apostle, Evangelist, Pastor, Teacher, or Prophet, if God wanted to introduce that person, He would use the noun "servant." In Isaiah 42:1, the Father refers to the Son (who had become "Son of man") as "my servant." You who have been called to serve God as an Apostle, or Prophet, or whatever it may be, if the Lord came to you, what do you think He would call you? I think He would address you as "servant." But how do you want the world to address you? Some ministers of the Gospel hate the word "servant." Do you enjoy (from the depth of your heart) being addressed as "servant"? The Lord said the greatest among His people shall be the servant of all (Luke 22:26-27). In admonishing His followers not to seek to share His glory, Jesus stated the following:

> *So likewise you, when you have done all those things which you are commanded, say, 'We are unprofitable servants. We have done what was our duty to do.'* (Luke 17:10, NKJV).

"Unprofitable" in these words of our Master implies deserving zero percent of the glory accompanying whatever He uses His followers to accomplish on the earth. "Servant" implies subjection to a Master to whom one owes all allegiance and operates only according to that Master's instructions. Therefore, nothing originates from the said servant and no glory should be attributed to that servant at any time. The said servant has no identity of his/her own, but is instead lost into his/her Master. Friend, reason with me a little. What do you think is the best title for a servant? If someone is a bondservant serving under a master, what is his best title? I suppose you would agree with me that the title that best fits him/her is "servant." Biblical titles are descriptors of the operations of God through His called servants and should not be sought for or clung to for honor of any sort. As you continue to enjoy the rest of this book, may you too be a servant of our Lord Jesus Christ in whatever area He has or is calling you to serve. May you never at any time seek His glory, as did Lucifer, who was consequently thrust out of heaven and became Satan.

CHAPTER 5

TITLEMANIACS AND RELATED QUESTIONABLE PRACTICES IN THE CHURCH

A few years ago in Buea, Cameroon, during a call-in program (*Showers of Blessing*) on Revival Gospel Radio, a servant of God called and introduced himself as Reverend/Doctor/Bishop ABC. He was someone we were familiar with, and at the end of his call the anchor of the program concluded the segment by saying, "That was Pastor ABC calling from Bomaka." This man was so enraged that he

Martin Tem

called back and corrected the anchor. This is what he said: "I did not say Pastor ABC, I said Reverend/Doctor/Bishop ABC."

This was a minister who did not have a church; he had something to the effect of a prayer room in the city. When he passed away about two years later, the handful of followers of his ministry pleaded with the Buea Gospel Ministers' Forum, to help contribute money so they could give the minister a minimal, modest funeral. This minister took a lot of pride in his titles but had absolutely nothing significant to show for them.

In another meeting, the coordinator introduced a minister as Pastor So-and-So, this minister wasted no time; he stood up immediately and said, "Point of correction, please. I am not Pastor... I am Reverend..." The love of titles has become a disturbing trend.

A few years ago, if you were called an Evangelist, you were shown great respect. Unfortunately, this is not so today; titles such as Prophet and Apostle seem to be dominating the landscape. If you successfully deliver two or three words of knowledge that are accurate, you can change your title to prophet. I have witnessed people trying to force God to speak to confirm their newly acquired title of Prophet. Even if the person being ministered to disagree with the 'prophet,' the prophet will say, "Think again, because the Lord cannot lie." As if this is not enough, there is another title that is beginning to take center stage in our midst, and that is the title of Bishop; some who take this title see themselves as Lords over God's Church, but how does the Bible describe a Bishop?

BISHOPS: OVERLORDS OR ELDERS?

When I took time to search the title of Bishop, I found that 'Bishop' is another translation for the title of 'Elder.' Don't take my word for it, do a search for yourself with the use of commentaries. Look up passages like Titus 1:1-7, and 1 Timothy 3:1-7:

Titus 1:4-8 (KJV) says:

> To Titus, mine own son after the common faith: Grace, mercy, and peace, from God the Father and the Lord Jesus Christ our Saviour. For this cause left I thee in Crete, that thou shouldest set in order the things that are wanting, and ordain elders in every city, as I had appointed thee: If any be blameless, the husband of one wife, having faithful children not accused of riot or unruly.

> For a bishop must be blameless, [it could equally read "for an elder must be blameless"] the steward of God; not self-willed, not soon angry, not given to wine, no striker, not given to filthy lucre;

But a lover of hospitality, a lover of good men, sober, just, holy, temperate.

One thing we should also take note of is that Bishop is not one of the five-fold ministry gifts. Apostle Paul asked Timothy and Titus to ordain elders in every town. Notice carefully that **Apostle** Paul asked **Pastor** Timothy and **Pastor** Titus to ordain **elders** who were also known as **Bishops** in every city. Paul gave that responsibility to Timothy and Titus, his spiritual sons in the ministry. Today we find pastors, evangelists, prophets, and apostles hunting for the title of Bishop at all costs. Is this not questionable?

Look at Philippians 1:1: *"Paul and Timotheus, the servants of Jesus Christ, to all the saints in Jesus Christ which are in Philippi, with the bishops and deacons."* Paul as an apostle was writing with Timothy to all the saints, with the bishops and deacons. Take note of the plural of bishops and deacons. Also take note of the sequence – bishops and deacons. The word, "bishop," is translated from the Greek word episkopos, which means a preaching elder. The Dakes annotated Bible, commenting on 1 Timothy 3:17, says bishop means a church officer, commonly called presbyter or bishop. Protestants are making something bigger of the office of 'bishop' simply to copy the way it used in the Roman Catholic Church.

A story is told of a preacher with the title of Apostle who went with his son to a government occasion. When the son introduced himself as Bishop, he was ushered in immediately. Since the government official at the door did not understand the importance of the title of Apostle, he refused the father entry. After this occasion, the preacher went and changed his title from Apostle to Bishop. Interesting, isn't it? This minister felt the worth of his title is based on the impact it created in the world, but is this the reason for titles in Church? Are we great in God's Kingdom because of how the world sees us?

The latest cankerworm or title-craze has been the hunt for honorary doctorates. There are now a number of ministers of the gospel, including those without the Ordinary (O' Level) or Advanced Level (A' Level) secondary certificate of education, who pay money to receive the title of "Doctor." We now have ministers introduced as "Doctor Pastor," but the English they speak is so poor that the world laughs at the Church as not knowing what we are doing. A minister once preached a message he took from one of my newspapers at a wedding in Nigeria. Some at the wedding proposed to give him an honorary doctorate degree for the message without realizing he had shared someone else's message.

CHRISTIAN LEADERS WITH THE RIGHT ATTITUDE TO TITLES

In Africa today, there are influential men of God like Pastor Enoch Adeboye, Pastor William Kumuyi, Pastor Chris Oyakhilome, and Pastor Matthew Ashimolowo, who have no other title but pastor. While some of them hold doctoral degrees, in church they prefer to be called Pastor. Pastor Kumuyi, for instance, has a doctorate degree, but he will only use it when he is writing on leadership for secular magazines like *NewAfrican*. In the church, however, you wouldn't know whether he has a doctorate degree or not.

Another man of God of distinction is Professor Zacharias Tanee Fomum (of blessed memory). Although he held the highest academic award on earth, the Doctor of Science, and was a professor of distinction, in church he was simply called Brother Zachs. This did not reduce his impact in the ministry in any way. There is Brother Gbile Akanni in Nigeria; his ministry is making an impact worldwide, yet he simply calls himself Brother.

The impact these ministers have in the lives of Christians all over the world has not diminished because they are not called Archbishop/Apostle/Prophet XYZ. Many do not even know that Pastor Enoch Adeboye of the Redeemed Christian Church of God (RCCG) is also a holder of a PhD in Applied Mathematics. This is because he does not parade it around as if this is what qualifies him for ministry in the Church. I don't have any problem with the title Bishop because it is biblical; my problem is the oversized self-importance attached to the office today by Protestants and Pentecostals, and the fanfare that goes along with it.

PENTECOSTAL BISHOPS COPYING NIGERIAN PRACTICES THAT IMITATE THE ROMAN CATHOLICS

I have asked myself this question many times, "Why is it that Apostle, Prophet, Evangelist, Pastor and Teacher, the offices given by our Lord Jesus to the Church, do not wear special robes, huge chains, small red caps, or a long caps with rings, but the Bishop has to put on all these things?" It became clear to me when I looked deeply into these things that even if our Pentecostal bishops try to defend their regalia with scriptures, it is clear that they are simply copying Bishops of the Roman Catholic Church.

I asked one of the Pentecostal Bishops in my country Cameroon, why all this fanfare about the title Bishop, and he told me that the Nigerian, late Bishop Benson Idahosa took the title because he saw that Roman Catholic Bishops who were not anointed like him had access to highly placed political leaders that he did not. So he decided to imitate them so that he too could have access to highly placed political leaders. This may sound reasonable enough, but the question I have is, "Why did he not remove this title once he had the access?" or "Why did he not limit its use to worldly matters?" Rather, he started using the title within the Body of Christ like a badge of approval by God, this practice has now become a negative legacy from him to the Church. Note that late Bishop Idahosa did not present any Biblical explanation for his actions, which has been copied by bishops today.

Another Cameroon minister who often goes to preach in Nigeria, said to me, "You haven't seen anything yet." He explained that he observed that to become a Bishop in Nigeria, a minister must have five Jeeps, he/she must have built a large house, he/she must have a church of at least one thousand members, and he/she should have at least 1 million Naira[4] in the bank. I did not verify this information, but if this minister is accurately reporting what he observed in Nigeria, I ask myself, "Where is the biblical backing for this?" My conversation with the Cameroon minister, helped me to understand why Nigerian preachers often have a speaking fee; and to understand why some come to Cameroon and use all manner of ungodly and dubious methods to raise money. This is terrible!

---

4   At the time when we had this conversation, 1 million Naira was worth close to US$10,000

In addition to regalia that Pentecostal Bishops have copied from the Roman Catholic System, they now refer to themselves as His Lordship, while others follow the footsteps of late Bishop Benson Idahosa, who before he died promoted himself to Archbishop. This is not limited to Nigeria and Cameroon, even in Ghana, some prominent ministers now append Archbishop to their names as we now observe when we buy their books. Where is the "Arch" coming from? Soon, we will have Pentecostal Cardinals and Pentecostal Popes. Once we have started going down their road, we will likely reach their destination.

In another conversation with another Pentecostal Bishop in Cameroon, I was told with great excitement that: "We are taking back what rightfully belongs to us." I asked him about the cap, the huge chain, and the rings, and he said, "Aaron had a special garment..." I asked him, "Why have we not also looked for some special robes or garments for the Apostles, Prophets, Evangelists, Pastors, and Teachers who are actually occupying an office Jesus gave to the body? Why do we only do it for Bishops?" He was a bit tongue-tied. I asked him, "do you know about the criteria to be consecrated a Bishop in Nigeria?" He winked and said, "That is another level." I told him, we have just started, every tree begins as a seed.

THE FIVE-FOLD MINISTRY: ARE THEY JUST A CATALOG OF PREFIXES?

The great desire for titles can have devastating consequences. It breeds pride and arrogance, it is therefore a destroyer of humility, a character trait highly desired by God. Those who search for titles often view the five-fold ministry offices as if they are just a catalog of prefixes to append to our names as we see fit. These individuals feel they can just rummage around until they find a title that satisfies their egos. If they sense that the title Apostle seems to carry more honor in society, they take it. If it is Prophet, they will instead go for that. There are many young ministers parading the title Apostle who have not successfully planted and established a church. There are many young ministers who do not even know what is expected of a prophet but they demand to be called Prophets.

Many of these young baby Apostles and Prophets have not learned that although you may have some apostolic traits or prophetic deposits or gifts, you must mature into an office. The Holy Spirit gives the gift, but the office is the recognition by the Church community over a period of time that a minister genuinely has that particular gift. These young ministers once they see or observe that they possess a gift, they grab the office corresponding to that gift immediately, though they have not yet been equipped to handle the responsibilities attached to the office they are parading.

Many of these young ministers have never considered that they must take time to study what is required of an office and if that office is really Biblical. Take for instance the common title of 'Reverend' – where is it coming from? It is not an office given by Christ to the Church. In some circles people will do anything, write any request, so that they can be elevated in position from Pastor to Reverend Pastor. Once they receive the title, you dare not refer to him or her as Pastor any longer or you will receive a severe rebuke.

When I talked about this title issue on the radio, a Brother from an evangelical church told me that some pastors are eager for this title because when they are transferred or appointed to lead a new congregation, and they have the title, 'Reverend,' they are able to negotiate for a higher salary, the title influences their pay. In my view, the problem with the title 'Reverend' is the source; it comes from the Roman Catholic system but it has now been adopted by Protestants as if it is biblical. Many Protestant ministers now believe that when they have served in ministry for a while, they deserved to be recognized as 'Reverend.' I am afraid that we find ourselves taking titles that are reserved for God alone.

Lately, I read a tribute in a book, the tribute was written by "***His Holiness.***" I was so shocked that I asked the author, "You allow a person to write a compliment in your book with the title His Holiness...?" I am very concerned that we are on a journey headed to somewhere unpleasant. If we don't retreat, we may be surprised at our destination. **I pray that everybody reading this should make an effort to read THE FINAL QUEST and THE CALL by Rick Joyner.** It may help us to see our present actions in the light of eternity.

Dear brothers and sisters, I have been mourning over this issue. I have felt pain when I see questionable practices invading the Body of Christ. The Bible says we know in part and we prophesy in part (1 Corinthians 13:9), maybe someone has a better insight from Scriptures that can calm my worries; I will welcome them. I don't have any problem with any individual anywhere, but I do have a problem with questionable practices. Have you heard new titles in Pentecostal circles today such as Archbishop, his lordship, his grace, his holiness, his eminence, apostle, arch apostle, prophet-bishop, senior apostle, senior prophet, arch deacon, arch elder, papa, mama, arch doctor, arch professor, arch pope, the right reverend, the very reverend, Reverend arch bishop, professor... some of these titles sound like bad jokes but you will be surprised to know that they exist.

TITLEMANIACS BREAK
FELLOWSHIP

In 2008, when the Full Gospel Mission (FGM) Cameroon conference IMPACT was going on in Douala, I met a friend whom I had not seen for a long time. Full of excitement, I went to him with a broad smile, as I stepped up to him with my hand outstretched, I greeted him "Hi Brother..." his reaction was astonishing. He did not even bother to shake my hand before retorting angrily, "I am Pastor..., I am not brother..., I am doing this to help you, you have to know how to show respect to your pastors." This happened in a crowd of people; if I state that I did not feel humiliated, then I would not be sincere to myself.

I later thought that it might have been good to tell him that I wasn't aware that he had been to Bible school and was now an ordained Pastor. Fellowship with my brother was broken because of his sense of pride and importance linked to his newly acquired title. There are moments when I feel like asking some title-obsessed people, "Why don't you carry a badge all the time with the inscription 'PASTOR,' or whatever title, so that no one would make the grievous mistake of calling you Brother instead of Pastor?"

I was pleasantly surprised at the reaction of Rev. Hal Rahman (founder of Discipling the Nations Ministry

(DNM) Cameroon with a proven track record as an apostle) when he came to Buea, and a young minister, young enough to be his biological son, called him Reverend. He said, "Call me Brother Hal. When you call me Brother Hal, it is more intimate than when you call me Rev. Hal." This is a man who has impacted many thousands of Christians all over Cameroon, who deserves a title, but he tells a young minister call me "Brother Hal."

It appears that as a minister goes deeper in his or her relationship with God, the less important titles mean to him or her. While some of our respected elders are letting go of bogus titles, many young ministers are instead concerned with getting the latest and biggest title they can lay hold off. These elderly ministers have come to understand that titles mean little without the life experience. It is the impact a minister has on people that really matters, not the title the minister carries. No wonder Dr. Mensa Otabil, the highly respected Bible teacher based in Ghana, says that mediocrity clings unto titles.

I once read about a preacher who was so title-obsessed, he was a real titlemaniac, so he decided to display his titles on a chain around his neck. The titles were the first three offices in the five-fold ministry. The initials were big and bold and placed vertically like this:

Apostle
Prophet
Evangelist

From a distance, the preacher's chain, read in bold letters the word '**APE**.' The hunt for titles does seem to make its hunters look like apes play-acting in a drama.

Today, in some churches or ministries, you must call the founder or leader Papa, Mama, Daddy or Mummy. I am not against respecting ministers, but in some of these settings, if you don't call that person a specific title, you are in trouble. Moreover, these practices in my opinion violate the spirit, if not the very command of Jesus, who said in Matthew 23:8-10: *"But be not ye called Rabbi: for one is your Master, even Christ; and all ye are brethren. And call no man your father upon the earth: for one is your Father, which is in heaven. Neither be ye called masters: for one is your Master, even Christ."*

I was told of a young minister in town who had taken the title of bishop. One of his members called him Pastor and he screamed at and humiliated the young man publicly for calling him Pastor instead of Bishop. That is the extent to which the love of titles is breaking fellowship. Instead of contently seeking first to be servant-leaders, instead of faithfully shepherding the flock, some are tragically first seeking for titles.

FROM PROTESTANTISM BACK TO ROMAN CATHOLICISM: IS THE JESUIT MOVEMENT RESPONSIBLE?

Do you realize that we are gradually bringing back what the Roman Catholics are doing, just with different names? They have holy water, we have anointed water, anointing oils, mantles, and many other practices that go beyond the practices of the people we protested against. If one observes how Pentecostals use anointed water and anointing oil nowadays, you would not disagree with me that is has become an idol in the Church. As far as this "bishop business" is concerned, one of our elders said he saw in a book where a Pentecostal bishop was greeting the pope while wearing a long cap. When we are carrying all these caps and huge chains, we actually cause the Roman Catholics to rejoice and mock us with sayings like "You left as a protestant but you are gradually coming back home." Why are we called Protestants when we are doing the very things we once protested against?

Could the Society of Jesus, popularly known as the Jesuit Movement, be responsible for these changes in Protestantism? The Jesuits are a missionary group in the Roman Catholic Church founded by Ignatius de Loyola, a Spanish soldier who became a priest, in August 1534. They work to expand the influence of the Roman Catholic Church publicly and behind the scenes. Protestants, including Pentecostals, in need of funding and other kinds of support to expand their work could unknowingly come under the influence of Jesuits. When protestant groups celebrate Ash Wednesdays, Good Fridays, and allow ministers to take on elevated titles and wearing of grand pastoral robes, one begins to wonder if the Jesuits are now in position to influence our protestant Churches – big and small. I wonder whether the members have even asked themselves the question of why the sudden change. It didn't just happen; someone worked day and night to make it happen.

Please, if you are reading this, do not to react with emotions; allow reason to prevail. I will welcome any feedback. Don't get angry! Anger stops you from rational thinking. Be rational and you will see the concern I have and why I have written this way. Let me close with excerpts from some emails I received when I first wrote this piece. I am grateful to these individuals who have graciously permitted me to share their views more widely.

I have been approached a number of times by co-workers suggesting titles but I immediately turn this down because I knew it is completely opposed to the Word of God. Much of what is happening today in the Pentecostal Church is a search for identity, ignorance, search for self-importance and self-respect, a total and intentional disregard for the Word of God and a search of belonging. Those who have chosen to hurt the Church of our Lord with such imported and fabricated titles must know that they will suffer the penalty in this life and in the life to come. This is no Joke. It is too serious.

Pastor Tinshu Genesis

The desire for titles is a mark of the Pharisees. This tendency is noticed with every immature believer, and is rooted in pride and self, with the end that we fall into the very sin that caused Lucifer to be banished from heaven. When I was a young Christian, I noticed the very signs in my own self. But thank God who rescues me from all these traps and forgives my sins. I frankly tell the few sheep in our congregation not to shy from calling me brother, after the Holy Spirit taught me that the most affectionate title in the kingdom is brother and the greatest title is slave of Christ…

Nicholas N. Ngepah

This is a great reminder for us to keep watch on the state of our hearts brother Martin. As one of our brothers said, the disease could be as old as the church itself. My first experience was about 15 years ago. I found myself in one of our big cities *in Cameroon. In need of help, I turned to **a very young pastor** (young in chronological age) and said, "Brother ..." (of course, I did not know he was a pastor). It was one of the church members who almost slapped me in the jaw. "How dare you call my pastor 'brother'?"*

Oteh Moses K.

With my experience since I traveled out of Cameroon, I have indeed seen that the respect for titles is a serious impediment not only to the African community as a whole but to the church as well. I agree with you that until we avoid this trapping that comes with titles, we cannot make meaningful progress spiritually and otherwise. The chasing of titles is like running after a shadow while neglecting the real thing and I think it is a new and effective weapon the devil is using against the body of Christ in these last days. This, if not stopped will limit the church of God. As you know, "Imitation is limitation."

Epie Njumbe

One of my cries is about the fact that many Nigerian "men of God" are creeping in gradually into Cameroon with so many ungodly practices and concepts about the ministry. Sadly, because of greed and covetousness most of our Cameroonian churches and their pastors are letting them. It is really terrible. This serves as lesson to us the next generation!

Matthew E. Otang

...we should balance this a bit - this should not take away from the decent respect that comes from acknowledging men of God. I see some young men call my pastor by first name for example... that may be OK for them but personally, that would be completely out of principle...(but that is personal) It just feels uncomfortable. In fact everyone calls my boss by first name - however, I asked him personally how he would like me to address him before I could do that. Now about the titles; call yourself whatever you want, and we will call you thus, just be sure that the title is not meant to project you ahead of the cross, so that people see you shining instead of the Messiah.

Ivo Teneng

CHAPTER 6

TITLES OPEN DOORS – ON THE ABUSE OF TITLES IN THE CHURCH

THE SECULAR EFFECTS OF TITLES

A title is a prefix or suffix added to someone's name, usually indicating one's achievement(s). Gospel ministers have a range of religious and academic titles at their disposal. Within a short period of time–starting in the late 90s and lasting through today–many African Gospel Minis-

Julius Ngwendson

85

ters of all calibers were observed to race one another for catchy titles. Recently, I initiated a discussion with a minister of the gospel on the phone after more than a decade of separation. My friend quickly wanted to know what title I go by now (thinking I own a ministry). I heard a disappointing tone in response when I told my friend I'm still called Brother Julius.

Secular recognition usually comes from one's title(s). Your titles may determine your interaction, recognition, and access. Society usually stratifies its people on the basis of academic attainment and financial status. Such social forces determine social honors and social interactions.

A GODLY HANDLE ON SELF-WORTH

Titles enable a quick assessment of an unknown person. Meeting for the first time, one is immediately identified and given due honor based on his/her title(s). As a result, it's commonly said that "titles open doors." Unfortunately, this notion has gained significant grounds among ministers of the gospel of Jesus Christ. The desire to use titles to open doors brings with it a desire for self-worth to many (a desire that was contrary to the Apostle Paul, who admonished us to follow Christ like he did). He had this to say about everything that made him worthy:

> *But whatever were gains to me I now consider loss for the sake of Christ. What is more, I consider everything a loss because of the surpassing worth of knowing Christ Jesus my Lord, for whose sake I have lost all things. I consider them garbage, that I may gain Christ and be found in him, not having a righteousness of my own that comes from the law, but that which is through faith in Christ— the righteousness that comes from God on the basis of faith. I want to know Christ—yes, to know the power of his resurrection and participation in his sufferings, becoming like him in his death, and so, somehow, attaining to the resurrection from the dead.* [12] *Not that I have already obtained all this, or have already arrived at my goal, but I press on to take hold of that for which Christ Jesus took hold of me.* (Phil. 3:7-12, NIV)

Paul the Apostle demonstrated the character of laying his achievements before his master, rather than picking them up. He followed the example of his master who stripped Himself of everything on His way to the cross:

> *Let this same attitude and purpose and [humble] mind be in you which was in Christ Jesus: [Let Him be your example in humility:] Who, although being essentially one with God and in the form*

of God [possessing the fullness of the attributes which make God God], did not think this equality with God was a thing to be eagerly grasped or retained, But stripped Himself [of all privileges and rightful dignity], so as to assume the guise of a servant [slave], in that He became like men and was born a human being. And after He had appeared in human form, He abased and humbled Himself [still further] and carried His obedience to the extreme of death, even the death of the cross! (Phil. 2:5-8, AMP)

This is an example of double humility by the Master Himself. Elaborating from Paul the Apostle, this mindset should be found in ministers of the gospel first before their followers.

SELF-EXALTATION VERSUS THE CROSS

With Jesus, exaltation was subsequent to His cross rather than preceding it (Phil. 2:9-11). Seeking titles is the same as seeking exaltation before your cross, which is contrary to our Master's example. One cannot carry his/her cross and his/her pride simultaneously. It was Jesus' Father who exalted Jesus, not Jesus Himself.

There is the temptation to desire titles for recognition, respect, and the opportunity to be heard. Titles may go further to enable the bearer to have his/her way on some occasions. It's worth bearing in mind that with recognition comes responsibility. Seeking the title of a Prophet, for example, may come with immediate gratification, but it will require the accountability of a Prophet on that great Day of the Lord. Thus, it becomes a responsibility to fulfill what the Father had in mind for giving that title to the church of His Son Jesus Christ. The more unprepared or unfit one is for a title, the more unpleasant his account will be on the day of accountability.

WHO'S RECOGNITION TO SEEK FOR AND WHY?

From a Scriptural standpoint, the mindset of Christians and Christian leaders is, or rather should be, different with regards to the acquisition and use of titles. Scripture teaches us to seek for the recognition of our Master as *"He* [Jesus] *must become more and more important, and I must become less important,"* (John 3:30, ERV). Our primary and main concern should remain to elevate Jesus Christ at every opportunity. This includes our characters, lifestyles, and titles. A servant of Jesus Christ should be recognized principally by the measure of God's grace in him/her, as allowed by the Holy Spirit rather than by his/her title. This glorifies Jesus Christ.

Scripture teaches that doors (opportunities, recognition, possibilities, etc.) are opened or shut by the Lord Jesus, not by titles:

> *Write this to the angel of the church in Philadelphia: These are the words of the one who is holy and true, who has the key of David. Whatever he opens, no one will shut; and whatever he shuts, no one opens.* (Rev. 3:7, CEV)

> *Write down My words, and send them* to the messenger of the church in Philadelphia. "These are the words of the holy One, the true One, and the One who possesses the key of David, which opens *the possibilities* so that no one can shut them. The One who closes *all options* so that no one can open: (Rev. 3:7, VOICE)

Using titles to open doors will lead one to doors that were not opened by Jesus Christ. Perhaps these will be the very ones who say to Jesus on the day of reckoning that they did this and that in His name (Matt. 7:22). Jesus says that He will reply to them plainly, "I never knew you. Away from me, you evildoers!" (Matt. 7:23) Also noteworthy is the Scriptural declaration that humility precedes God's open doors, "Humble yourselves before the Lord, and he will lift you up." (James 4:10)

As an act of humility, a Servant of Christ may want to wait for the confirmation of his title from two or three reverent ministers as witnesses (II Cor. 13:1). Grabbing a title can be detrimental to one's ministry, as can accepting one blindly. This can be as dangerous as setting the wrong foundation.

Some titles are duly earned, while others are cheaply given. Servants of God with earned titles serve in their roles by the grace of God and abound in fruits thereof prior to being given those titles. Their titles were fruits because "you can tell each tree by its fruit," (Matt. 7:20, NIRV). They walked in their titles before they were entitled. On the contrary, those who seek titles walk behind those titles, and that is walking in darkness. They grab their titles, and then do all they can to manufacture the fruits in keeping with them.

WHAT THE ABUSE OF TITLES INCLUDES

The proliferation of institutions and ministries in this day and age has made it possible to have almost any qualification and/or title one desires. The abuse of titles in the church includes (i) the rush, (ii) grabbing of the wrong titles (including titles reserved for God alone)

(iii) the multiplicity of titles, (iv) using titles as rewards, (v) using titles to retain membership, and (vi) using titles for favoritism.

The rush.

People rush to acquire titles due to impatience or peer pressure. Jesus advised His followers not to identify a plant when it's still too young, for fear of misidentification. Equally, when a tree starts to bear fruits, it's best to allow them to come to full maturity before harvesting. Harvesting fruits that are immature usually leads to detrimental consequences; nobody enjoys unripe fruits. Addressing yourself by a title sets an expectation that can be met only with the maturity of your experience with the Lord Jesus Christ. This is a tall order for someone walking behind his/her title(s). Not meeting those expectations brings abuse to the title and the work of Jesus Christ. This is why Paul cautioned Timothy not to elevate an unfit person to leadership in the church too quickly. "Do not be hasty in the laying on of hands, and do not share in the sins of others. Keep yourself pure." (1 Timothy 5:22)

Taking the wrong title.

Many have been lured into taking titles upon themselves that are unfitting. Being at the helm of one's ministry and not accountable to a higher authority is unhealthy. One would likely struggle with a wrong title, because the elements of the title do not flow naturally. This error happens for two reasons: people desire to be recognized for what they aren't, and people want the attention of crowds for fame. Seeking recognition through titles brings glory to the flesh as it indulges in "the pride of life and the lust of the flesh" (I Jn 2:16, KJV). The desire for recognition is vanity itself. Attracting crowds the wrong way exposes them to fleshly manifestations. Scripture teaches that if we sow to the flesh, we will reap corruption. *"For he that soweth to his flesh shall of the flesh reap corruption; but he that soweth to the Spirit shall of the Spirit reap life everlasting."* (Gal. 6:8, KJV) It's like dressing in the attire of a police officer but going to war like a soldier.

Having multiple (undeserved) titles.

The grace of God is upon some of His servants who are multitalented, some of who do not even go by a single title. However, it would seem others believe in the worldly saying, "the more the merrier." They seem to believe the more titles and/or the bigger one's titles, the greater the anointing, influence, and accomplishments one may have. It doesn't take too much effort for one to come across titles like "Great Minister," "Senior Apostle," "Senior Bishop," etc. These titles are a clear exaggeration, and a sense of departure from the doubly humble example set forth by the Lord Jesus Christ. It can be argued that Jesus was humble, but also had many titles. It's important to note that He laid down *everything* on His way to the cross, as cited earlier (Phil. 2:5-8). In the same way, every follower of His still on earth *should* be on his/her way to a cross. "⁴Then Jesus told his disciples, 'If anyone would come after me, let him deny himself and take up his cross and follow me.'" (Matt. 16:24, ESV)

Using titles as rewards.

Some titles are acquired as rewards, rather than as a call to serve in those offices. This gives a sense of accomplishment, which is completely contrary to the mindset of Jesus Christ and the Apostle Paul in Phil. 2:5-8 and Phil. 3:7-12, respectively. Regarding a title as an accomplishment makes one expected to be served and to be somewhat at ease in Zion, something Scripture forbids (Amos 6:1). The church is a vineyard for laborers, rather than a society for accomplishments. True followers of Christ have their rewards in heaven (Matt. 5:12).

Using titles to retain membership.

There have been a number of experiences whereby a new member, usually well positioned in the society, becomes part of a church. Within a short time, he/she is appointed and ordained with a title. The newly ordained brother or sister becomes responsible and doesn't leave the church anytime soon. This usually leads to novice leaders that the Apostle Paul warned about; that a leader should

"[6] not [be] a novice, lest being puffed up with pride he fall into the *same* condemnation as the devil." (1 Tim. 3:6, NKJV). Who is responsible in such cases? Both the appointer and the appointee will be accountable before the Lord. One should be free in his/her spirit to turn down any such offer until the right time.

Using titles for favoritism.

Favoritism is showing kindness to a person or group over others with equal claim; it is synonymous with partiality. There have been instances where an authority in the church liberally elevates his proponents to positions with certain titles. Young graduates from Bible colleges have been quickly elevated to positions with titles because of their relationships with someone in authority. Our Lord had this to say when He thought of all these disappointments: *"But when the Son of Man comes, will he find this trust on the earth at all?"* (Luke 18:8B, CJB) The Lord is looking for those who are selfless enough to turn their backs to favoritism in the vineyard.

CONCLUSION

The Devil's weapon to abuse titles in the church has become so effective due to our negligence. In the world, it can be accepted that 'titles open doors,' but as children of God, it is imperative to erase the notion that titles opens doors. God is the one who opens doors, and He is able to provide whatever is needed for ministry, including honor:

> *For the Lord God is a sun and shield; the Lord bestows favor and honor. No good thing does he withhold from those who walk uprightly.* (Ps 84:11, ESV)

We must fix our minds on Jesus Christ and not on titles: "Therefore, preparing your minds for action, and being sober-minded, set your hope fully on the grace that will be brought to you at the revelation of Jesus Christ." (1 Pet. 1:13). The abuse of titles in the church will be minimized if every Christian commits his/her mind to these principles.

CHAPTER 7

CONCLUSION

The Word of God is the foundation of everything about God. It teaches us about God's character, His attributes, and His plan of salvation for man. According to 2 Timothy 3:16-17: *"All Scripture is given by inspiration of God, and is profitable for doctrine, for reproof, for correction, for instruction in righteousness, that the man*

Hermann Donfouet

of God may be complete, thoroughly equipped for every good work." Thus, our lifestyle, attitude, behavior, and teachings should be based on the Word of God, not the style and the doctrines of the world. With regards to the use of titles in the Body of Christ, we must seek God's position on the matter. In other words, how does God think about the use of some titles such as Archbishop, Cardinal, His

Holiness, Reverend, Superintendent, Bishop of Bishops, Apostle Prophet Doctor of Nations, and so on? God has not left us orphans.

His Holy Spirit through His Word gives us answers; God has exalted His Word above His name (Psalm 138:2). The prophets, kings, and men of God of the past loved the Word of God and always referred to His Word on all matters relating to God and man. But these days, many beloved brothers, sisters, and men of God set the Word of God aside. Many have lost their first love and are engaged in a frantic search for titles. Worldliness and other devilish influences have infiltrated the Church with certain titles that are not scriptural, and this deeply wounds the heart of God. Unscriptural titles exalt the self and take us away from God. If nothing is done, many beloved brethren may not enter into Heaven.

The current book discusses titles in the Church of God and warns children of God about the wrongful use of them. Having observed the negative impact of titles being used in the wrong way in the Body of Christ, fellow Christians of various denominational groups decided to speak out through this book. Some chapters may have touched you. The purpose of these chapters is to produce humility and prepare you, the reader, for the imminent return of the Lord. Do you have in your heart a keen desire to do only the will of God? Is there a flaming fire in your heart to serve God without brandishing your titles? Do you have a strong desire in your heart to let God build his throne in your heart and not your titles? If your answer is "yes," then this book will do you good. You will no longer be the same after reading it. A deep desire to serve God in humility will burn in your heart.

Have you forsaken God by being caught up in the hysterical search for titles and recognition of men? Have you wounded brothers and sisters because they forgot to call you Pastor, Bishop, Superintendent, Cardinal, Reverend, or Elder? Are you enrolled in a theological university or any other university in order to gain a title that, according to you, will open your doors in the ministry? Are you hurt, bruised in your heart, and even angry when brothers and sisters just call you "brother" or "sister"? Beloved, we invite you to probe your heart in the light of the Word of God and His Holy Spirit. It may be that you are far from heaven because you have deeply hurt the Lord and the Body of Christ by using your title like a hammer to knock others down. May the Lord open your eyes, give you the grace to repent and walk in His light. We love you and may you be ever blessed.

REFERENCES

Dickens, Charles. 1837. Oliver Twist.
Richard Bentley Publishers. Chapter 37,
online: http://www.gutenberg.org/files/730/730-
h/730-h.htm#chap37 [accessed 26 January 2016]

Joyner, Rick. 2006. The Final Quest.
Morningstar Publications

Joyner, Rick. 2006. The Call.
Morningstar Publications

Ogden, Greg. 1990. The New Reformation:
Returning the Ministry to the People of God,
Grand Rapids: Zondervan

Piper, John. 2002. Brothers, We Are Not Professionals:
A Plea to Pastors for Radical Ministry.
B&H Publishing Group

Ryle, John Charles. 1977.
Expository Thoughts on the Gospels, Vol.1,
Grand Rapids: Baker Book House Reprint

The Society of Jesus. 2016. Our Mission.
    Online: http://jesuits.org/mission [accessed 26
    January 2016]

Tozer, Aiden Wilson. 2009. Reclaiming Christianity:
    A Call to Authentic Faith, Baker Publishing
    Group

Warren, Rick. 2002. The Purpose-Driven Life.
    Grand Rapids: Zondervan

Authors Biographies

Rev. Dr. Daniel SHU (MD, MAOL, DL) is specialized in Radiodiagnisis, an ordained minister of the Gospel, a writer and a university lecturer. Since 2000, he has held the post of the President of the Medical Board of the Full Gospel Mission Cameroon. For 12 years, from 2002 to 2014, he served as Pioneer Haggai Institute Regional Director for Francophone Africa. Today, he is pioneering LEAD Higher Institute a university plant in Yaoundé Cameroon. He also serves as a consultant in leadership and marriage counselling. Daniel has been married to Elizabeth for 30 years. They have five lovely children who support them as they travel widely investing their lives to build lives.

Eric Tayem Tangumonkem, Ph.D. holds a Bachelor's degree in Geology and a minor in Sociology from the University of Buea in Cameroon, a Master's in Earth Sciences from the University of Yaounde in Cameroon, and a Doctorate in Geosciences from the University of Texas at Dallas. In addition to being a Geoscientist at Denbury Resources, he is an Independent Certified Coach, Teacher and Speaker with The John Maxwell Team and also the CEO of IEM APPROACH LLC, and President/ co-founder of Equipping of the Saints International Ministries based in Dallas, Texas. He is married to Elizabeth Tangumonkem and God has blessed them with five children; Afaamboma, Nstongmboma, Elotmboma Abuetmboma and Atseamboma.

Emmanuel O. Nuesiri, Ph.D. has been teaching the Bible in a bi-vocational capacity for close to 30 years. He is an alumni of the Philip Project UK, and works with Pastors desiring to move beyond superficial engagement with the Bible, by building their capacity in expository and inductive Bible study. Emmanuel holds a PhD. in Environmental Governance from St. Antonys College, University of Oxford. He is a research affiliate at the University of Illinois Urbana Champaign, USA, and a research fellow at the University of Potsdam, Germany, working on climate change governance. He is married to Joyous Tata and they have two children.

Patrick Tamukong, Ph.D. is the founding Pastor of the US Full Gospel Mission in North Dakota, U.S.A. He is a Bible Teacher by calling and author of *"Restoration: The Ernest Desire of Our Lord Jesus Christ for His Bride."* Patrick holds a Ph.D. in Theoretical and Computational Chemistry with a Minor in Quantum Physics from the University of North Dakota, U.S.A. He is currently a post-doctoral research associate at North Dakota State University, U.S.A. He is married to Delphine Banjong and their union is blessed with two beautiful daughters (Shekina & Pearl).

Tem Martin is a journalist, researcher, motivational speaker, writer and entrepreneur. He has been actively involved in the transformation of society through his books and seminars on entrepreneurship and financial empowerment, goal setting and time management, preparing singles for marriage among others. He is the C.E.O of Productive Living Inc. Ltd, an enterprise involved in training, coaching, capacity building, printing and publishing of books. As a writer, he has written and published over 20 books. He is married to Rachel, who is a stronger supporter of his career and ministry. They have been blessed with a daughter, Treasure-Noela, and a son, Zionson.

Julius Ngwendson (Ph.D. and Pastor) is an Instructor of Chemistry at Normandale Community College in Bloomington, Minnesota USA. Brother Ngwendson studied at the University of North Dakota from 2003 to 2008. During that time, by God's grace, he led the effort to found the TACC-Friends Association, an association of children of The Apostolic Church Cameroon in the USA. He's been the founding President from 2011 to 2015. Today, the TACC-Friends Assoc. has branches in the UK, Thailand and Canada. Bro. Ngwendson also led efforts to found TACNAM (The Apostolic Church North America Mission), an organization for churches being planted as extensions of The Apostolic Church Cameroon. He also found an online forum for children of the Full Gospel Mission Cameroon in the diaspora, among others. Bro. Ngwenson is married to Gloria Ayuck for 13 years and they're blessed with three boys : Joshua, Kaleb and Micah.

Dr. Hermann Pythagore Pierre Donfouet t is a born again child, Spirit-filled Christian who loves God and His Church. In November 2015, he joined the research laboratory: Economy and Social Sciences, Health Care System and Societies in Marseille-France as a health economist. His research focus is primarily on health economics, environmental economics and applied spatial econometrics. Scholarly works by Dr. Donofouet have been published on European Journal of Health Economics, International Journal of Health Care Finance and

Economics, Health Economic Review, Environment and Development Economics, Empirical Economics to name a few. Dr. Donfouet is happily married to Gaëlle Laure. They have two children: Peniel and Othniel.

IEM PRESS

Inspire, Motivate & Equip

To order additional copies of this book call:
214-908-3963
or visit our website at
www.iempublishing.com

If you enjoyed this quality custom-published book,
drop by our website for more books and information.

"Inspiring, Equipping and Motivating Publishing"